The Lynton & Barnstaple Railway

Yesterday and Today

by

P. Gower, B. Gray & K. Vingoe

THE OAKWOOD PRESS

© Oakwood Press & P. Gower, B. Gray and K. Vingoe 1999

British Library Cataloguing in Publication Data
A Record for this book is available from the British Library
ISBN 0 85361 537 3

Typeset by Oakwood Graphics.
Repro by Ford Graphics, Ringwood, Hants.
Printed by Cambrian Printers, Aberystwyth, Dyfed.

Also available from the Oakwood Press:

The Lynton & Barnstaple Railway by L.T. Catchpole
Lynton & Barnstaple Railway, An Anthology, by D. Hudson & E. Leslie

Available from the Oakwood Video Library:

The Lynton & Barnstaple Railway
featuring the L.T. Catchpole Collection

Front cover, top: Woody Bay station after closure in the 1930s.   *R.N. Bishop*

Front cover, bottom: Woody Bay station in the late 1990s.   *Paul Gower*

Published by
The Oakwood Press
P.O. Box 13, Usk, Mon., NP5 1YS.

Contents

This circular plaque is mounted on the building that now stands at Castle Quay, the site of Barnstaple Town station platform. *See page 11.*

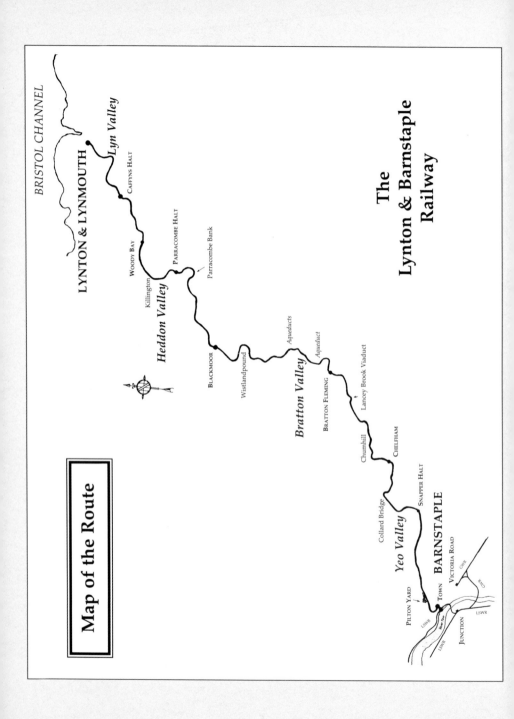

Map of the Route

The Lynton & Barnstaple Railway

BRISTOL CHANNEL

Lyn Valley

LYNTON & LYNMOUTH

CAFFYNS HALT

PARRACOMBE HALT

WOODY BAY

Parracombe Bank

Killington

Heddon Valley

BLACKMOOR

Wistlandpound

Aqueducts

Bratton Valley

Aqueduct

BRATTON FLEMING

Lancey Brook Viaduct

Churnhill

CHELFHAM

SNAPPER HALT

Collard Bridge

Yeo Valley

BARNSTAPLE

PILTON YARD

TOWN

VICTORIA ROAD

GWR

LSWR

LSWR

LSWR

GWR

JUNCTION

Preface

With closure of the Lynton and Barnstaple imminent, Leslie Catchpole and Roger Kidner, together with Michael Robbins, decided to produce a book on the railway. Published by Oakwood in 1936, *The Lynton and Barnstaple Railway* is still in print today, many years after the closure of the line. Leslie Catchpole never wrote another book as no other railway meant that much to him. That fascination with this long closed railway still affects people today and the passage of time only seems to create even more interest in the L&B.

In the 1930s, there was an unofficial L&B Appreciation Society with several well-known railway enthusiasts communicating with each other. One of them, Frank Box had such affection for the line that he moved to North Devon. One can only imagine his feelings after the closing of the L&B as the day after the sale he moved away. In 1937, a year after the closure, W.E. Hayward, Colling Turner and Stanhope Baker, together, visited and photographed the line. Also, many authors inspired by the L&B put pen to paper and David Hudson and Eric Leslie have gathered some of these together in *The Lynton and Barnstaple Railway, An Anthology*.

Over the years the fascination of the L&B has not waned. There are now several books and regular articles in the railway press. There is some ciné film, a wonderful legacy of photographs and numerous details left by those who knew and loved the line when it was operational.

There are some that are opposed to England's premier narrow gauge line being awakened from its slumbers, saying that they prefer to remember the L&B as it was, (whatever that might mean, as few of them ever knew it). But today there is a new generation of admirers who want to experience the joys of a line that they never knew. Fortunately Exmoor is much as it was in the 1930s, having seen little development over the intervening years.

The Lynton and Barnstaple Railway Association was formed with the intention of gradually restoring the L&B just as it was. The Association has purchased Woody Bay station; in almost original condition and in one of the few possible locations capable of accommodating modern day tourist requirements, it is a perfect place from which to start what some have dubbed 'Mission Impossible'. However, railway enthusiasts have already proved that the impossible is just that which has not yet been attempted. An original coach is in the final stages of being rebuilt and another is underway. Even an original goods van, thought to have been burned long ago, has been found and is being restored. With a Manning, Wardle locomotive scheduled for completion within the next three years, it can be seen that the restored L&B will be far more than 'a spluttering petrol tractor clattering along a few yards of reclaimed industrial trackage'.

Stanhope Baker once said of the L&B 'You can't describe it really, but it had an atmosphere all of its own, it was delightful'. How right he was.

Introduction

That the Lynton & Barnstaple Railway has reached its centenary of its opening rather more publicly than most former Southern Railway branch lines is mainly due to its narrow gauge, which was probably also one cause of its demise. It is also a tribute to a small band of enthusiasts who discovered the charms of the line in the early 1930s, one of whom, Leslie Catchpole, wrote the first history of it, published by the Oakwood Press in 1936.

Their enthusiasm was in vain. The line had several disadvantages; the terminus was too high above the village; a coastal bus service instituted by the railway, later became a serious competitor; the carriages were somewhat heavy, leading to some expensive double-heading; and it had no mineral traffic. But it did have wonderful scenery, which ironically is one argument against its now long-planned re-opening, as the Exmoor authorities fear its spoiling. It is hard for readers to imagine a narrow gauge railway spoiling anything; perhaps some others will decide from this book that it did not look bad in its former state.

I myself first travelled on the line in 1929, blissfully ignorant that in a mere seven years it would be gone. I sincerely believe that one day it will be there again.

R.W. Kidner
1999

Leslie Catchpole with camera in hand stands on the platform at Lynton. Taken by his friend and colleague Roger Kidner in 1934.

Authors' Note

Since closure 63 years ago, much of the trackbed of the L&B has reverted to private ownership. A book such as this could only have been produced with the co-operation and consent of the present owners of the old right of way, many of whom showed interest and were helpful in our project. The re-opening of part of the L&B has been the dream of many for a number of years; today we stand on the threshold of reinstatement and this has only been achieved by courtesy, discussion and consent. Turning the dream into a reality is hard enough and we are sure you would not wish to make the task even more difficult by alienating the present custodians of the trackbed and environs. The authors respectfully ask that you acknowledge the rights of the present landowners by not trespassing.

Acknowledgements

We would expressly like to thank Roger Kidner for not only making photographs from his private collection freely available to us, but for graciously agreeing to write the introduction. As one of the founders of Oakwood Press, who produced the first book on the L&B all those years ago, we can think of no one more suitably qualified to link the past with the present.

We owe much to those who photographed and documented the L&B over its short life. Particularly, Leslie Catchpole, Roger Kidner, Frank, Donovan and Charles Box, H.C. Casserley, Humphrey Household, Ken Nunn, A.B. MacLeod, H.F. Wheeller, R.L. Knight, Stanhope Baker, W.E. Hayward, Colling Turner and R.K. Cope, for without them this book would not have been possible.

Mention must be made of the present caretakers of photographic collections, as not only do they maintain many irreplaceable photos of the L&B but also allow public access to this rich heritage. In particular, Roger Carpenter, Les Franklin and the staff at the North Devon Athenaeum Barnstaple, John Smith of Lens of Sutton, Graham Stacey of the LCGB and Steve Knight of Knight's Photographers Barnstaple.

We would also like to thank the L&BRA, the Lyn and Exmoor Museum, Bill Gould, Nigel Hearn, Richard Hoyland, Colin Pealling, Bill Pryor, John Rodgers, Colin Shears and John Travis for loaning us rare photographs from their private collections. Thanks also to Eric Leslie for allowing us to use his 100th anniversary artwork.

Our gratitude and thanks to the following individuals and organisations who assisted us in our endeavours whilst in North Devon to photograph the present. Mr and Mrs Adair, Mrs de Casas, Court Estates, the Crocombe family, Exmoor Inns, Mr Kellaway, Mr and Mrs R. Maddocks, Mr and Mrs D. Moore, Mr and Mrs Pile, Mr and Mrs W. Pryor, Mr and Mrs C. Saddington, Mr Sanders, Mr and Mrs Shaw, Mr and Mrs L. Wooder and from Lynton, the Sefi Family for transport arrangements and Pat and Trevor Ley for accommodation above and beyond the call of duty!

Barry and Paul took the present day views. Barry also produced all of the prints and designed and photographed the back cover. Keith and Paul researched the photographic locations and compiled the captions.

Staff pose for the photographer on the steps at Barnstaple Town station in the early years of the railway. The station cost about £6,000 to construct of which the LSWR contributed only £2,000, the remainder coming from the L&B. The first station master was F.C. Watkin, who was previously porter-in-charge at Barnstaple Quay station. A listed building, the station is at present unoccupied. *Courtesy L&BRA*

All is brand new - The Barnstaple Town station was constructed by W. Gibson of Exeter and was a replacement for Barnstaple Quay station, which closed the day the L&B opened. It was intended that an arrival platform would occupy the area on the left but as this was never built, the site was used by railwaymen as an allotment. Today the trackbed is part of the Civic Centre car park. *NDA*

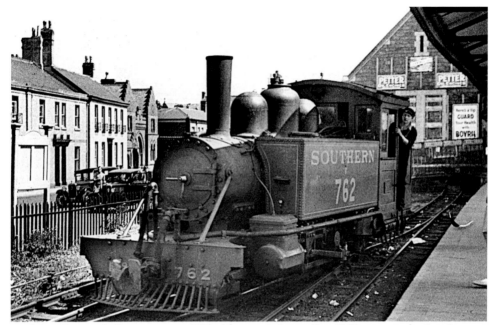

Lyn at Barnstaple Town, summer 1935 with passed cleaner Ronald Sprague on the footplate.
The last survivor of 90 American locomotives imported at the close of the 19th century, she was
the only American engine to run on the Southern until after World War II. In a few months she
will be sold at auction for £50 and scrapped.   *Lens of Sutton*

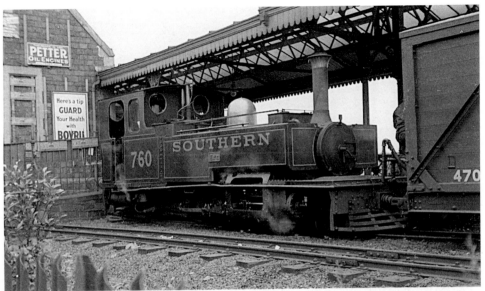

Exe at the buffer stop on Saturday 17th August, 1935 after working the 6.05 pm from Lynton. Although overhauled and repainted during the winter of 1934/35, *Exe* will fetch only £34 at auction because she is fitted with a steel firebox. Today the stop block on the head shunt is still there and on the building at Castle Quay, which now covers the site of Barnstaple Town station platform, is a circular plaque, which commemorates the L&B, and its terminus.   *H.F. Wheeller*

Left: The wrecking crew at Barnstaple Town transhipment siding in 1936. After closure, the rail layout was modified to facilitate removal of redundant material. In the foreground is an 8-ton bogie open, which is part of the wrecking train. The wall in the present view (*above*) is part of the Barnstaple flood defences.   *E Northcombe*

Built in 1899, Messrs Stanburys' Victoria Flour Mill dominates this view of Rolle Quay. The River Yeo and Rolle Quay were a bustle of activity in the early part of this century and contributed greatly to the wealth of the area. At one time, Rolle Quay handled 100,000 tons of traffic yearly. Stanburys' Mill was demolished in 1983 and today there is very little traffic on the river or industry on the quay. Today flood defences form the edge of a car park.   *F.E. Box*

The track after closure, between Town and Pilton on 24th August, 1936. At this point trains would slow to the mandatory 8 mph before crossing Braunton Road. Some of the sleepers are concrete which were laid by the Southern in the mid-1920s as part of improvements to the track. The hipped-roof building links the past with the present. On the left, Braunton Road swing bridge has since been replaced with a fixed span and the trackbed in the foreground is now home to a cycle rack and car park. *R.K. Cope*

The track looking back towards Town station on 17th May, 1937. In the distance the track curved to a radius of under 3 chains. In the background is the L&B signal box at Barnstaple Town; the station is behind the buildings on the left. The garage on the left and the building on the right of the crossing are the only features that appear to have remained unchanged since the railway closed.   *Colling Turner*

Taken the same day in 1937, this photograph of the crossing gates at Braunton Road shows that the road was considerably wider than the railway. On the right, close by the crossing was a hut where a bell instrument was kept to inform the crossing keeper of train movements. The turnout for the quay siding was just behind the photographer. Today the road has been made even wider and the remaining building in what was once Gould's Yard has just undergone extensive refurbishment.   *Colling Turner*

The provision of quay accommodation on the Yeo, in line with that provided by the Ilfracombe Railway on the Taw, was a requirement of Barnstaple Town Council. Contractor's locomotive *Excelsior* prepares to return to Chelfham to collect spoil from widened cuttings in that area. This was required to facilitate works between there and Barnstaple Town station. The culverts now bricked up were for the Mill Leat, which ran beside Pilton Yard and the Mill Wheel tailrace and were apparently the source of a dispute between the mill owner and the railway company.

NDA

Pilton Crossing 1937. The foundations and steps of the L&B's centre of activity, Pilton signal box can be seen through the level crossing gates. Track materials over the level crossings were specifically excluded from the sale. Although the yucca plant obscures the view, the gatepost caps are still there although the right-hand gatepost has been moved to accommodate modern transport needs. *Colling Turner*

The rear of Pilton Yard changed little over the intervening years as this photograph, taken in the 1980s, shows; from left to right the buildings were goods shed, carriage sheds 1 and 2 and the loco workshop, which was at the back of the engine shed.   An extensive fire on the 8th September, 1992 damaged the buildings beyond repair and the site has now been cleared and is in use as a car park. The remaining building is Sanders Sheepskin shop, which was formerly the L&B Company office.   After the Southern took over the line, the offices became surplus to requirements.   *Keith Vingoe*

Looking toward Pilton crossing gates May 1937. Just out of sight, to the right of the crossing gates was the location of Pilton signal box where all trains exchanged tablets. S. Castle, the Plymouth ship breakers, who dismantled the line, left the yard loop and track to Barnstaple Town *in situ* after *Lew* left Barnstaple on the18th September, 1936 bound for the King's Dock, Swansea. Ten days later aboard the SS *Sabor*, *Lew* left for Brazil and oblivion. Today the Civic Centre dominates the background. *Colling Turner*

Pilton Yard in June 1935 and all looks well. The coach on the left, L&B No. 17, has just returned to the yard after forming part of the first up train of the day. Built by the railway company in 1911 and costing £453, in a few months it will be cut up for garden sheds. *Taw* shunts stock on the adjacent road, later that year she will be sold for £50 and scrapped. Today, only the L&B offices, which have reverted to their original ownership, and the oil store on the left, which was a Southern addition, remain to remind us that this was once a railway depot.   *S.W. Baker*

Pilton Yard 1913. This 4-ton open wagon, No. 10, was involved in a serious accident at Chumhill in February 1913. The wagon is shown here in Pilton Yard, on No. 2 Loco Shed road adjacent to the inspection pit, shortly after the damage to the upper planking sustained in the accident has been repaired. The backs of the houses have changed little in 60 years.   *R.L. Knight*

At the end of the headshunt at Pilton Yard in 1936 are Lot No. 67 the match truck and behind
Lot No. 66 one of the two cranes bought from George Cohen and Sons by the Southern in 1926.
The match truck was reconstructed from a third crane by the Southern at Lancing Works in 1927.
To the right can be seen the truncated main line. Today all is overgrown and the land unused
(*right*).   *R.N. Bishop*

Mill Leat looking towards Pilton before the opening. The track is brand new and in the distance is Pilton Yard. It is hard to imagine the developments that have taken place in this quiet backwater of Barnstaple. The fence posts cast in Exmouth Junction Concrete Works still stand although the right-hand post has succumbed to the forces of gravity. The buildings on the right are sheltered accommodation for the elderly and beyond them are the backs of the houses in Yeo Vale Road. *NDA*

The permanent way is being laid towards Barnstaple in the Yeo Valley. Rail destined for this location was loaded onto barges and floated up the river. The total weight of the rail used to build the line, 1,320 tons, arrived at Fremington in three 440-ton lots from Workington Cumbria aboard the SS *Lancashire*, at that time the largest ship to have ever used Fremington Dock. Today the river bridges are gone and the lower reaches of the Yeo are just wasteland.   *NDA*

Dismantling at bridge No. 10 in the spring of 1936. The rails of 30 ft in length were loaded on to one of the 8-ton bogie flats. The bridge, which had two spans of 12 ft, was blown up in the 1940s as part of a war exercise. Today the banks of the river are heavily scoured and the river at this point is now over 35 ft wide. The pole in the background indicates the route of the trackbed.

R.W. Kidner

The wrecking crew had a rota for stacking the sleepers and, in the spring of 1936, Fernleigh Hutchings stands in 8-ton bogie open No. 28303 on this duty. Quite often when the engine started all the sleepers would be inadvertently rearranged. The trackbed today is clear and Southern Railway concrete fence posts are still in place.   *Bill Gould*

Just further north, five of the wrecking crew hold a length of rail. They are from left to right, George Morgan, Bill Gould, Fernleigh Hutchings, Vincent Hearn and Edward Thorne. This photograph was taken by the sixth member of the crew Nelson Marshall using Bill Gould's camera. The redundant rail, which fetched 42 shillings per ton, was cut into 10-foot lengths and melted down at Port Talbot Steelworks. Although at this location the fence posts are gone, little development has taken place to change the view. *Nelson Marshall*

The track bed approaching Snapper Halt with Yeotown in the background. Taken two years after closure from the adjacent road, few people today would know that the railway ran this close to the road at this point.   *Colling Turner*

Snapper Halt was the first stop out of Barnstaple. Not in the original prospectus, it first appeared in the timetable in 1903. Constructed after requests from the village of Goodleigh, which was over half a mile away, trains stopped here only by request and never after dark! The shelter still stands and attracts mainly bovine attention these days. *L&GRP*

Southern Railway coach No. 6991, L&B coach No. 1 (an observation brake composite), was left at Snapper Halt after closure. Built by the Bristol Wagon and Carriage Works and costing almost £397 when new, it realised no more than £13 10s. at auction. After falling into disrepair, it was eventually burned.   *Lens of Sutton*

The track curves away from the Halt through the hamlet of Snapper, towards Chelfham. Just 17 chains north from here a serious derailment occurred on Friday 29th August, 1924. The 6.20 am from Barnstaple had just left Snapper when van No. 23 derailed due to rail spread. It took just over four hours to clear the line. The brake column from 6991 was dumped on the trackside near cattle creep No. 15 at 2 miles 61½ chains from Barnstaple and remained there for many years. Today the rhododendrons have taken over.   *Lens of Sutton*

In this view from a hillside above Snapper, the location of both of the coaches left on the trackbed after the railway closed can be seen. Interestingly none of the wrecking crew can remember how the coaches got there! In 1959, the coach furthest away from the photographer Southern Railway coach No. 6993, originally brake compo No. 15, was removed by the then infant Festiniog Railway. After modifications, the coach has now run for more years on that line than it did on the L&B. The today photo shows how little the view has changed.   *R.L. Knight*

Taken before the opening, a train is on the embankment between the River Yeo Bridge and Collard Bridge. This photo was used on the front of L&B timetables and on advertising materials. A hand-tinted version was included in the official postcard set initiated by C.E. Drewett who was General Manager of the L&B from 1899. Just off to the left is another locomotive to take the train back to Pilton, as this was the extent of the permanent way at this time. Nowadays on the other side of the river there is a Scout camping ground. *NDA*

The embankment from the other side with the first up train of the day on the 12th August, 1935. *Taw* heads towards Barnstaple with a seven-compartment third and observation brake composite No. 17. Looking at this view of a train in the landscape it can be easily understood why the L&B is so popular with modellers with kits available in almost all of the scale/gauge combinations for nearly all of the stock.   *R.W. Kidner*

A down train from Collard Bridge. Taken by Roger Kidner in the summer of 1929 whilst on a family holiday, this is one of the very first photographs he took of the L&B. It is the first down train of the day and the loco is believed to be *Exe*. *R.W. Kidner*

View of the trackbed north of Collard Bridge after closure. The cutting in the distance leads to Northleigh Road bridge known locally as Skew bridge. It has been documented that the contractor had difficulty in laying out the line in this area. However, it is safe to assume that this was not the preferred route and that the contractor had little choice but to cross under the road at this point. The local council, unimpressed with the road layout, informed the company that if they had known that the bridge was to have been constructed as it was, they would never have given their consent to the modifications to the road. It is not surprising that shortly after closure, the road was returned to its original route and the bridge bypassed. More recently, the track ballast has been taken to shore up a nearby riverbank.   *R.K. Cope*

Excelsior is facing downgrade towards Barnstaple on Goodleigh Road bridge with a load of spoil destined for Barnstaple. This bridge is interesting inasmuch that the abutments are of masonry, rather than of the brick used for the other road bridges on the lower section of the line. The contractor, James Nuttall of Manchester, commenced construction of this bridge and Chelfham viaduct sometime shortly after March 1896. The Southern rebuilt the upper part of the bridge in concrete. A substantial structure, it is likely to remain for some time.   *NDA*

Chelfham viaduct. In 1895 the Consulting Engineer Sir James Szlumper estimated that £2,600 was enough to build all the viaducts on the line, Chelfham alone is said to have cost £6,500. The single most expensive piece of engineering on the L&B, it is constructed of Marland bricks on masonry piers.

Chelfham viaduct is a Grade 2 listed structure and is currently owned by the privatised successors to the British Rail Property Board. Standing 70 ft high with eight arches each of 45 ft and at 132 yards long, it is also the largest narrow gauge viaduct in the United Kingdom. Due to the buildings underneath, it is difficult to dismantle, so it will probably stand for many years as a lasting reminder of the L&B.

Taken from the cab of a Manning, Wardle at the Northern end of Chelfham viaduct by a lady on holiday from Cheltenham. The crew of the engine, driver Frank Northcombe and fireman Frank Nutt, allowed the lady and her companion to ride on the footplate and take turns at firing. The view up the valley is still as it was. *Miss M. Rayment*

Chelfham station has been described as one of the prettiest in England. The station building was small but still contained a waiting room and ticket office as well as the electric train tablet machine. Withdrawn at auction when bidding went no higher than £275 it was later sold by private treaty and today is a private residence. Although the railway has gone, the ambience is still the same.   *W.W. Dunning*

Saturday 28th September, 1935, trains pass at Chelfham. The fireman of the 10.15 am down is handing the single line tablet to the porter signalman as the station master looks on. The loco crews will change trains here with the up crew returning to Lynton and the down crew returning to Barnstaple. It is now a sylvan glade. *R.W. Kidner*

The rear of Chelfham station in 1937. The wooden extension was a Southern addition. It still looks the same today.   *Colling Turner*

Chelfham to Bratton Fleming

29th September, 1935. The last down train pounds up the 1 in 50 on the bank at Loxhore just north of Chelfham. The train left Barnstaple at 11.50 am after connecting with a half-day excursion from Ilfracombe and Torrington. As can be seen, contrary to some published reports, the down trip enjoyed bright sunshine for this part of the journey. Apart from the lack of track, little has changed. *R.L. Knight*

Loxhore looking the other way as the last train passes. In the observation compartment of the last coach F.E. Box records his final log of a down journey on the L&B. Frank Box travelled on the L&B over 100 times and completed 65 logs of his journeys. E759 *Yeo* was always his favourite and so great was his affection for this engine that when the railway closed he obtained *Yeo's* Southern Railway number plate and Manning, Wardle works plate and had them fastened to his study wall. *R.L. Knight*

On 26th February, 1913, four men of the Bratton Fleming track gang were riding in 4-ton wagon No. 10 when at about 8 am the wagon gained such speed that it could not be checked by application of the brake. The wagon loaded with leaves and other debris collected from trackside cesses, left the line at Bridge No. 25 near Chumhill Farm and plunged 20 feet into a field. It can be seen here before recovery at the foot of the bridge. The bridge still stands.

R.L. Knight

The track gang repack the ballast on the bridge. Of the four men riding on the wagon, George Barrow, aged 57 was killed outright. William Welch, aged 36, suffered a fractured skull and died a few days later on March 2nd. George Kirby who lived in a now demolished cottage near Chumhill took brandy to the injured. The deceased were buried in Bratton Fleming Churchyard. *R.L. Knight*

The two men not killed, foreman ganger, George Dymond and F. Dinnicombe, attributed the accident to wet leaves on the line. Interestingly they were in possession of the single line token at the time. Recovery of the wagon was achieved by means of a chain attached to an engine, the wagon being pulled up the bank. The locomotive used was *Yeo* fitted with a modified cab, and judging from the new paint on the smokebox door and chimney on a running-in turn after her winter overhaul.   *R.L. Knight*

Behind the engine is one of the L&B's original brake vans of 1898 in use as a mess van, and against the wagon with his back to the camera is W. Leatherby, Pilton carriage and wagon examiner. In the background is Bratton Cross road bridge and just the other side of this is the quarry from where the stone was extracted for the masonry piers of Chelfham viaduct. Today although the quarry is overgrown, it is still evident and the road overbridge still stands.

R.L. Knight

Bridge No. 30 was Lancey Brook viaduct (*left*). The second viaduct on the line was a curving structure 50 yards long and 28 ft high with eight 15-foot steel spans on masonry piers. During his inspection carried out on Wednesday 4th May, 1898, Colonel Yorke of the Railway Inspectorate insisted on extra girders being installed under the decking for extra stability in case of a derailment on the viaduct, work to be completed within three months of his inspection. This location is now very overgrown and a present day comparative view would show nothing of interest, so the today view shows the trackbed on the embankment approaching the site of the viaduct from the north (*above*).   *L.T. Catchpole*

Lancey Brook viaduct was not in the original prospectus. Theories for its construction include that the area was too wet for an embankment, that there was not enough fill available, and that the hillside was too steep for anything other than a viaduct. In the early 1940s, sometime after closure, the viaduct was blown up, along with some of the river bridges, as a war exercise. All was destroyed apart from the northern buttress wall, which still exists. However, just south of the viaduct a platelayers' hut can still be found.   *L.T. Catchpole*

Yeo on the 10.15 am from Barnstaple crossing cattle creep No. 31 on the approach to Mill Lane bridge, also known as Pennyall bridge. This is early summer 1935 as the rear coach is a freshly repainted 6991, the coach which ended its days at Snapper Halt. The driver is Wally Worth and the fireman is Ernie Heale. Mill Lane bridge has gone but the embankment and cattle creep at Pennyall Farm is still there. *Ernie Heale Collection*

Bratton Fleming was the largest village *en route*, 1,000 yds from and 185 ft above Bratton Fleming station. Because of width restrictions the station was cut into the bank and consequently, unlike the other stations, the goods yard faced the down loop, so goods vehicles for Bratton had to be marshalled at the rear of down trains. In the foreground is the turnout for the goods yard and in the distance is the seldom-used water tank.

NDA

Bratton station building was unique in having a small glazed porch, and standing by it in this view is the L&B's longest serving station master John James Baker. Originally the regular driver of Jones Brothers horse-drawn Lynton to Barnstaple coach, which ceased running when the railway opened, he took up the post of station master at Chelfham on 6th June, 1898, moving to Bratton Fleming on 21st September, 1904. When he retired on 30th September, 1931, his wife became station attendant under the jurisdiction of the station master at Blackmoor. Mr Baker still frequented the station and was photographed handing the station books over to the guard of the last train. Mrs Baker left the company's service on 30th September, 1935, the day the railway closed. The station, sold at auction in 1938 for £100, is today a quiet private residence.

Bratton goods yard 1935. On the left is the goods shed and in the foreground the location of the siding which was removed in February 1932, along with the passing loop. From then on vehicles would have had to be shunted either by hand or by horse. The upturned skip is a relic from construction so is over 37 years old. Today the goods shed is gone and the yard area is a private garden.   *A.B. Macleod*

North of Bratton looking towards Button Hill bridge No. 35. The fence posts dated 1913 were cast in Bratton goods yard proving that the L&B used concrete long before being taken over by the Southern. The large concrete gatepost is new and has been cast *in situ*. Just beyond the gatepost is the location of a subterranean water tank. Bratton station already had a water tank but locomotives could not be watered whilst the train was at the platform, so the L&B built this tank, but it was never connected to a water column. Today it forms the foundation for a shed.

R.L. Knight

The 10.15 am ex-Barnstaple approaches Button Hill Bridge on 11th August, 1927. *Lew* is the pilot and *Exe*, which is in the intermediate livery that was also applied to *Yeo* at this time, is the train engine. Humphrey Household, the photographer who had been walking the line, must have had a bit of a scramble to secure the location for this photograph, as the cutting is narrow and the walls steep. Today the track may be narrower but an engine still steams up the 1 in 50 occasionally.

H.G.W. Household

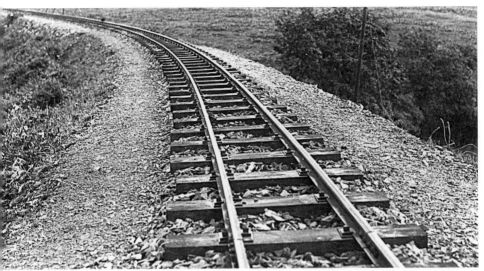

Freshly re-laid track on Bratton Bank in 1927. The Southern also reduced the cant as they thought the L&B's was excessive. However, these modifications initially contributed to derailments and after some further modifications to the track, most of the problems were solved. The bank whilst not high or as long as others north of this location is still impressive and standing well. The route is still clear although gorse bushes predominate. *H.G.W. Household*

Lew with the 6.07 pm ex-Lynton approaches Bratton Fleming on the 8th September, 1933. Although credited elsewhere as Hunnacott Bank it is actually Bratton Bank looking south. The today photograph is taken from further back to avoid foliage masking the comparison.

LCGB/Ken Nunn Collection

There were four aqueducts between Bratton Fleming and Blackmoor. Two have disappeared, but this one, No. 37 rebuilt in concrete, still stands at 8 m. 20 ch. Because of a shortage of fill for the several banks in this area, many of the cuttings on this section are much wider than required for the passage of a narrow gauge train. Currently farmers and their dogs use the aqueduct as an improvised and perilous means of crossing the cutting.   *Oakwood Collection*

A demolition scene at Narracott bridge No.39. The crew are nowhere to be seen so are probably at lunch in van No. 23. Because of heavy snow disrupting milk collections, in the 1960s the trackbed north of the bridge was put to use as a road serving farms at Sprecott and Hunnacott. Today it still serves this purpose.   *L.T. Catchpole*

Trolleying down from an inspection at Wistlandpound. When this photograph was taken in 1898, the construction of the railway was a year behind schedule. Settlement in this very wet area was causing serious delay and the Engineer was forced to accept a short grade of 1 in 29. Interestingly, Colonel Yorke made no comment about this during his inspection. Across the background can be seen the trackbed heading towards Blackmoor. Today, the water of Wistlandpound Reservoir covers most of the site of the horseshoe curve.   *NDA*

These two photographs show the last train on Wistlandpound Bank on 29th September, 1935. In the first photograph, the train is at the foot of the 1 in 29 with both engine's regulators open for the climb. The gradient was short, certainly no longer than 100 ft, so could be easily rushed by down trains. The second view shows the last train on the highest part of Wistlandpound Bank. This huge earthwork was removed in the 1950s during construction of the reservoir. However, just behind the photographer is Bridge No. 52, which still stands.   *(Both) R.W. Kidner*

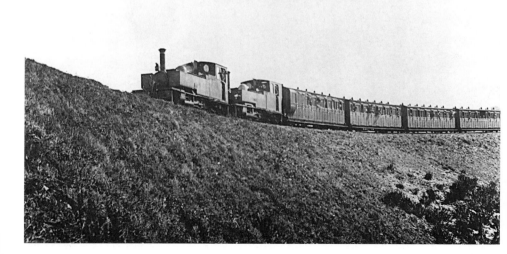

The last train approaching Blackmoor at 11 m. 49 ch. crossing the tallest occupation bridge on the line, Bridge No. 55. Having climbed 8 miles at mostly 1 in 50 from Collard Bridge, the longest stretch of 'collar work' will be over at the top of the 1 in 75 at Blackmoor. Today the view is much the same. *R.L. Knight*

A view of Blackmoor with Charles Drewett, General Manager of the L&B from 1901, standing next to the ground frame cabin. Although this picture, taken in the early years, is credited at the bottom as Blackmoor Gate station, to the railway it was always Blackmoor station. In the very early days, the station sign read Blackmoor for Parracombe. At 913 ft above sea level, this was the first summit of the line. *Major, Darker and Loraine*

Blackmoor station in 1937 is derelict and boarded up. Later it will be sold at auction for £700. To the right can be seen Blackmoor Gate Station Hotel where Leslie Catchpole stayed when he came to North Devon to film the last train. The hotel was demolished after a fire in 1970. *R.N. Bishop*

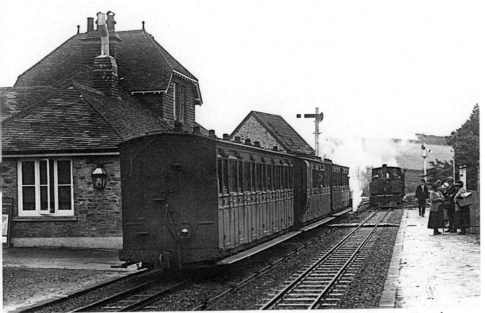

Trains crossing at Blackmoor. One of a collection of photographs taken by Humphrey Household on a damp Thursday 11th August, 1927. *Taw* waits in the up platform with a three-coach train as *Yeo* arrives in the down loop where some of the concrete sleepers installed by the Southern can be seen. After the long climb from Collard Bridge, coal in the fireman's side bunker would be getting low so it was not uncommon at Blackmoor to see loco crews standing on the tank tops transferring coal across the boiler top from the driver's side bunker.

H.G.W. Household

Lyn taking water at Blackmoor. The base of the water tower housed a hot air engine and its exhaust pipe can be seen by the window. Manufactured by A.E. & H. Robinson of Manchester, the hot air engine was used to pump water up from a sump into the water tank, which also served the water column on the up platform.   *Lens of Sutton*

The Blackmoor water tank was a product of W.C. Rafarel of Newport Foundry, Barnstaple. After closure, the tank was pulled off the top of the tower and scrapped. The overbridge was removed during road improvements, but the base of the water tower still remains and the station building has been tastefully extended and is now a thriving restaurant.

P. Gower Collection

The last train from Barnstaple on the downgrade below Hollacombe Farm. The footplate crew on *Lew*, the pilot engine, were driver Dick Cording and fireman Freddie Worth. The train engine was *Yeo* with driver Wally Worth and fireman Ernie Heale. E.S. Moore and A.E. Edwards together with other Southern top brass accompanied the crews on the footplate for the last trip. The trackbed is difficult to identify in the present day view. *R.L. Knight*

Taken from the Parracombe bypass shortly after completion late in 1927, this view of Rowley Bank shows the track heading towards Parracombe. During construction this area was proposed as a site for Parracombe station and in the very early days was the last place that engines of down trains could take water, obtaining it from a rather inadequate contractor's water tank. Today it is difficult to recognise the location because of the growth of trees.

Robert Brain Collection

Between Rowley and Parracombe, No. E759 *Yeo* heads a train across Bridge No. 59, Holwell occupation bridge. The first vehicle is van No. 56041, better known as L&B van No.23. Last used on the demolition train in 1936 it was thought to have been burned long ago. However it was discovered in a field near Georgeham and is now being restored by the Bristol Group of the L&BRA. Today, although the span has gone the remains of the bridge abutments are still there and the view has changed little.   *Lens of Sutton*

Parracombe

An up train on Parracombe bank in the late 1920s with the recently-opened Parracombe bypass and Highley Farm in the background. During the night of the Lynmouth flood disaster in 1952 water collected in the space between the two embankments due to a blocked culvert under the railway embankment. This eventually gave way causing damage and additional flooding in Parracombe. Although very overgrown, the remains of the bank can still be identified today.

E.A. Sweetman

Parracombe Bank from the recently completed Parracombe bypass. At 50 ft high and 8 chains long it contained a sixth of the total material excavated over the whole line during construction. The bank took a year to build and 3 ft-gauge track and rolling stock was employed in its construction. Thirty years later, 6 tons of explosive were used during the construction of the bypass, so one can be sure that much more effort was required to build the railway.

Robert Brain Collection

Lyn and *Exe* head a heavily loaded up train towards Parracombe Bank on a summer Saturday evening in 1935. *Lyn* was usually the pilot when trains were double-headed; possibly, because her shorter fixed wheelbase and equalised suspension gave greater freedom on curves. In addition, her inside Stephenson link valve gear had a less disruptive influence on train oscillations. Today the right-hand gates and posts of the accommodation crossing have gone but those on the left survive. The track bed can be identified by the line of gorse bushes leading into the cutting.   *H.F. Wheeller*

Yeo on the 10.15 am from Barnstaple approaches Parracombe, some distance before the halt. The buildings on the left, of which one was a corrugated iron Chapel, are on the far side of Parracombe bypass. It has often been said that the bypass contributed to a decline in railway passenger traffic. However, the Lynton bus still went via Parracombe so did not use the bypass. Today a bungalow stands on the site of the Chapel, the profile of the trackbed can be seen as a line through the gates, and the Lynton bus still goes via Parracombe.   *Lens of Sutton*

Another view of *Yeo* with the 10.15 am train approaching Parracombe in the summer of 1935. Taken from the other side of the track and a little closer to the halt than the previous view, the crew are both on the driver's side for the benefit of the photographer. Today the posts are still there either side of the trackbed to indicate the route. As Parracombe had no goods siding, although there was one in the early days, wagons for Parracombe were detached from down trains and left on the track to be collected on the way back and pushed all the way to Blackmoor!

Paul Gower Collection

The 10.15 am ex-Barnstaple train taking water at Parracombe. The water stop here was essential as there was none at Woody Bay and the supply at Lynton was unreliable. The locomotive is easily recognised as being *Lew* as she was the only engine to have been fitted with four cab ventilators. Initially these were fitted inside and consequently let in the rain but were soon modified no doubt after complaints from the crews about getting wet! A substantial bungalow and stable block now occupy most of the site.   *A.B. Macleod*

The Southern concrete replacement for the original wooden shelter taken shortly after closure. The halt at Parracombe first appeared in the timetable in 1899 and in the early years a porter walked down the line from Blackmoor to dispense tickets. In later years, train tickets were made available at Parracombe Post Office. Although looking forlorn the shelter is still there today.

R.N. Bishop

The safety valves lift as a down train leaves Parracombe. Behind the train is St Petrock's Church whose Rector, the Reverend Chanter, (the brother of the L&B's resident engineer Frank Chanter) is credited with spreading flower seeds along the line. However, one of his legacies is an abundance of that pernicious plant, Japanese Knotweed, which has overtaken certain parts of the line. Perhaps he should have heeded the maxim 'As ye sow so shall ye reap'. Today this quiet wooded glade can still conjure up images of a narrow gauge train.

LCGB/Ken Nunn Collection

A double-headed down train, almost certainly the 10.15 am from Barnstaple heads under the Killington Road overbridge. The locomotives are No. E760 *Exe* and No. E761 *Taw*. The coalbunkers on the fireman's side of both locos are almost empty so coal will have to be transferred from the driver's side bunker at Lynton. This area is now used by the local council to store road and drainage materials.
Lens of Sutton

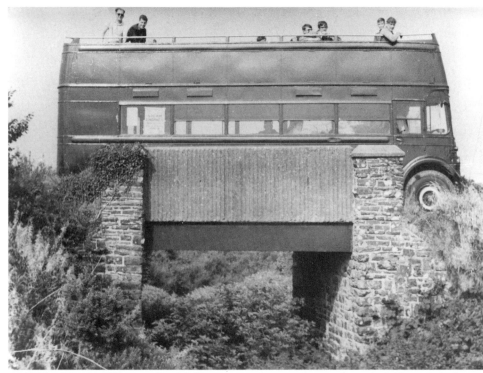

Bridge No. 65, Killington Road bridge, was unique, as it was the only bridge originally constructed with trough decking. It was later partially rebuilt with concrete parapets. In the mid-1960s a group of bus enthusiasts used JK 5605, an ex-Eastbourne Leyland Titan 'TD4' (still in its livery of Civil Defence Department dark green) to tour the route of the L&B. It was fortunate that someone decided to photograph the bus on this bridge, otherwise we may never have known what it looked like, as today the bridge has been completely removed and the site cleared. Today, the fence posts on the right help identify this location.

Colin Shears Collection

The management of the L&B, being keen to show off their railway, arranged for a reporters' train to travel over the line on the 9th March, 1898. Frank Chanter, Evan B. Jeune and others of the party pose at Woody Bay for the photographer Mr Loraine. Apart from the track and the train, the view still looks the same.

NDA

This evocative photograph of the 10.15 am ex-Barnstaple arriving at Woody Bay shows what a beautiful location this is. At 964 ft above sea level, it was the highest Southern Railway station 1923/35. The view looks out towards milepost 15½, the point to which the Southern removed the track in November 1935. Again, it can be seen that little has changed to affect the view over the years.   *R.L. Knight*

As a young boy, Humphrey Household visited the line in 1915 and persuaded his father to take this photograph of Woody Bay for him. Twelve years later he returned to take his own photograph of the station. Built by Jones Brothers of Lynton on land given to the railway by Benjamin Greene Lake who eventually ended his days in prison for fraud, Woody Bay was the only station, apart from the terminus stations specifically, mentioned in the Act of Parliament which authorised the L&B, and according to the Act was to be 'forever efficiently maintained'. That the Southern hastily removed the track from Lynton to a point past Woody Bay after closure seems to lend credence to the opinion that the railway was closed in defiance of the Act of Parliament. *(Above) H.G.W. Household/(Below) L&GRP*

Woody Bay, the only station building still largely in original condition, is now owned by the Lynton and Barnstaple Railway Association and is considered by many to be one of the most beautiful locations for a station anywhere. The scaffolding was erected in the spring of 1998 so that Devon Group Members of the L&BRA could carry out roof repairs which were completed shortly after these photographs were taken. The scaffolding has now been removed.

The approach road to Woody Bay station on 23rd August, 1936. On the left is a Southern Railway private road notice. Unfortunately, the approach road is unsuitable for modern vehicular needs and alternative access to the station is to be arranged. The trees planted by the company shortly after the opening to shield the station from view still surround the station today and add much to the attractiveness of this location.   *R.K. Cope*

A group of hikers consult the map at Woody Bay Top. The road on the left leads to Woody Bay itself. At least 1¾ miles from Woody Bay station, it was intended that a branch line would be built connecting with a cliff railway at the terminus. Neither was built and today thankfully, much remains as it was.   *P. Gower Collection*

When Stanhope Baker took this view in 1935, close to the highest point of the line at 980 ft above sea level, it was inconceivable that in five years, almost to the date, gunfire would be heard in the skies over this tranquil location. World War II came to North Devon in earnest on 24th July, 1940 when three 'Spitfires' shot down a 'JU 88' German bomber. The plane eventually crashed close to the trackbed on Martinhoe Common. The two crew members who survived the crash were captured without incident and taken to Lynton police station. Today all is tranquil once more and the trackbed can still be identified curving around to where a caravan sits on the formation in the distance. *S.W. Baker*

New Mill Halt was opened in December 1906. Later renamed Caffyns Halt its main service was to golfers destined for Caffyns Golf Links. On a grade of 1 in 50 up, crews of Barnstaple-bound trains would be reluctant to stop here anyway. The site of the halt was cleared away in the 1980s but the route of the trackbed can still be seen running into the cutting in the distance.

R.W. Kidner

With the road removed from either side, New Mill Lane bridge at Caffyns is open to the elements and is slowly crumbling away, but at least we can see how it was constructed.

R.N. Bishop

The Clubhouse at Caffyns Links, also known as the Lynton and Lynmouth Golf Club. The well-known photographer of the L&B, F.E. Box is known to have played golf here. Because of its location, the rules make for interesting reading. Today the links are no longer in use and the clubhouse is a ruin.   *J. Stanley (Lynbridge)*

The track heads away down the 1 in 50 from New Mill Lane bridge towards Dean Steep road overbridge. There are stories of a platelayers' trolley, stored at Woody Bay, being used on this stretch of line as a quick means of returning to Lynton by off duty railwaymen and their families on Sundays. It was, of course, an unofficial means of travelling! Just to the left can be seen the road to Lynton which runs parallel to the track at this point. *Colling Turner*

Dean Steep road overbridge broadside looking towards Lynton. This bridge forced the road into a dangerous 'S' bend. After closure, the bus company implied that it intended to use double-deckers on the Lynton run so the bridge was removed and Dean Steep reprofiled. However, no double-deckers were ever used on this route. The trackbed can be seen on the left of the road as a slight rise in the roadside verge.   *R.N. Bishop*

From the other side of Dean Steep road overbridge looking towards Barnstaple. The modifications to the road layout after closure can be clearly seen and today the site of the original road overbridge approach road is now the lay-by on the left. *L&GRP*

Dean Steep from the hillside looking towards Lynton. The embankment was removed in the 1940s to extend the runway at RAF Chivenor.   Dean Lane bridge, No. 77, was removed along with the embankment. The line of gorse bushes helps to show where the trackbed lies in the deep and narrow cutting leading towards Lynton.   *Gunn's Gallery, Lynton*

A train at Dean Steep from the hillside looking towards Barnstaple. On the left can be seen allotments and to the rear of the train a platelayers' hut built into the wall of the cutting. Today the remains of the platelayers' hut are still there and just in the foreground are the angle irons on either side of cattle creep No. 78. *Valentines/Courtesy Jean Le Bombe*

Larkscleave Bridge No. 80, the first bridge out of Lynton, with a Barnstaple-bound train. The loco is *Exe*, which can be identified by the raised ejector pipe. This was a modification forced on the company after certain fittings had been stolen from the locomotive whilst in store in a barn in Barnstaple before the opening. High above Fountains Cross the bridge is still there. *Frith's*

The 6.05 pm from Lynton crosses Larkscleave on Saturday 17th August, 1935. Photographed from the train by H.F. Wheeller who came to Lynton by paddle steamer to travel on the line just once before its closure the following month. The two locos are working hard on the beginning of the 1 in 50 out of Lynton. Today the area is a shady walk. *H.F. Wheeller*

A train leaves Lynton sometime in the 1930s. To the left are three carriages in the bay road. The ground frame and signals are Southern replacements. To the right is the engine shed built by Jones Brothers for £150. Today a garage occupies the trackbed and to the right a house has been built on the site of the loco shed. Behind the house, the coaling stage still exists.

P. Gower Collection

The station master's bungalow at Lynton. Ernest Bentall, of the well-known department store family from Kingston-upon-Thames resided here after the railway closed. An admirer of the line he took several photos, some of which have been published. The wagon is a Howard 8-ton bogie open, delivered new to the railway on 11th August, 1927.   *J.G. Hoyland*

Lew shunting at Lynton summer 1935. To the left is the coal siding and to the right under the station trolley is a weighbridge. The points at this end of the station were all hand thrown and not interlocked. When the railway opened the turnout faced the other way but this was soon changed to facilitate shunting. The view towards the goods shed is much the same, but the locomotive is unlikely to be required to do any shunting in the near future.   *A.B. Macleod*

LYNTON

Lynton station, 700 ft, above sea level and 200 ft above the town of Lynton seen after the station master was provided with the bungalow on the bank opposite the platform and the Southern enlarged the station buildings. The gates are still there, but it has been a good few years since any passengers' luggage came through them. *L&GRP*

View of Lynton station exterior after closure. Withdrawn at auction in 1938 when bids stopped at £475, it was later sold by private treaty and is now a private dwelling. The small windows are for the extra toilets installed when the station building was enlarged. However, as the water supply was still unreliable they often remained closed. The road on the left was not built until 1922 although it was promised that it would be built soon after the opening. The sign on the wall declares that it was once Lynton's railway terminus.   *L&GRP*

Lynton goods shed was built by the local firm of Jones Brothers, who also built the station buildings here and at Blackmoor and Woody Bay. Although the goods traffic to Lynton consisted mainly of coal, amongst other goods traffic received and forwarded were parcels, cans of milk, general goods and minerals. Obviously built to last, since closure the goods shed has been converted into two attractive cottages. *L&GRP*

A triumphal arch commemorating the Cutting of the First Sod on 17th September, 1895 on the road to Hollerday House, Sir George Newnes' residence above Lynton. On the left is the site of Lynton Town Hall a gift to the town from Sir George. The contract to construct the Town Hall was awarded to Jones Brothers of Lynton. The foundation stone was laid on the 11th May, 1898 as part of the official celebrations to celebrate the opening of the L&B.   *Frith's*

Another triumphal arch at Lynton commemorating the Cutting of the First Sod. Hollerday House, which unsurprisingly was also built by Jones Brothers, can be seen through the arch. The road through the arch leads to the Valley Of Rocks Hotel, where the opening was celebrated in 1898. A hundred years later, the Lynton and Barnstaple Railway Association celebrated the Centenary of the opening at the same hotel.   *Frith's*

List of Bridges

Courtesy of L&BRA

Photographed by Roger Kidner, Leslie Catchpole takes his ciné camera back to his car as the last train heads under Wistlandpound occupation bridge (No. 52) towards Blackmoor on 29th September, 1935.